REVISED AND UPDATED

Transportation
Around the
World

Motorbikes

Chris Oxlade

Heinemann Library
Chicago, Illinois

P9-AOI-133

Customer Service 888-454-2279
Visit our website at www.heinemannraintree.com

Designed by Kimberly R. Miracle, Ray Hendren, Cavedweller Studio and Q2A Creative
Printed in China by South China Printing Company

12 11 10 09 08
10 9 8 7 6 5 4 3 2 1

New edition ISBN-10:   1-4329-0202-4 (hardcover)
                        1-4329-0211-3 (paperback)
New edition ISBN-13:   978-1-4329-0202-5 (hardcover)
                        978-1-4329-0211-7 (paperback)

The Library of Congress has cataloged the first edition as follows:
Oxlade, Chris.
        Motorbikes / Chris Oxlade.
                p. cm. — (Transportation around the world)
        Includes bibliographical references (p.   ) and index.
ISBN 1-57572-305-0 (library binding)
1.   Mopeds — Juvenile literature. [1. Mopeds.] I. Title. II. Series.

TL443 .O95 2001
629.227'5 — dc21

                                                              00-010064

Acknowledgments
The publisher would like to thank the following for permission to reproduce photographs: R.D. Battersby pp. **4**, **6**, **15**, **17**, **23**; Corbis pp. **12** (Reuters), **27** (Zefa/Jon Feingersh); Eye Ubiquitous p. **20**; Getty Images p. **13** (The Image Bank/Moritz Steiger); PA Photos p. **29**; PhotoEdit p. **24** (Dennis MacDonald); Pictures p. **25**; Quadrant pp. **9**, **11**, **14**, **18**, **21**, **22**, **26**; Science and Society Picture Library p. **8**; Tony Stone Images p. **19**; Travel Ink p. **28** (Tim Lynch); TRH Pictures pp. **5** (Gilera), **7**, **10**, **16**.

Cover photograph of a motocross rider reproduced with permission of Getty Images (Jim Arbogast).

Every effort has been made to contact copyright holders of any material reproduced in this book. Any omissions will be rectified in subsequent printings if notice is given to the publisher.

Contents

Some words are shown in bold, **like this**. You can find out what they mean by looking in the glossary.

What Is a Motorbike?

A motorbike is a machine with an **engine** that moves along on two or three wheels. There is a seat for a rider, and sometimes for a passenger. People call some motorbikes "motorcycles," or just "bikes."

engine

A motorbike does not need a lot of space to park.

helmets

handlebars

These riders are safely enjoying riding their motorcycle.

The rider steers a motorbike to the left or right using the handlebars. Controls on the handlebars make the motorbike go faster or slower. The rider should always wear a helmet for safety.

How Motorbikes Work

Most motorbikes have two wheels. Each wheel has a **rubber tire** around it. The tires grip the road and stop the motorbike from sliding sideways as it goes around corners.

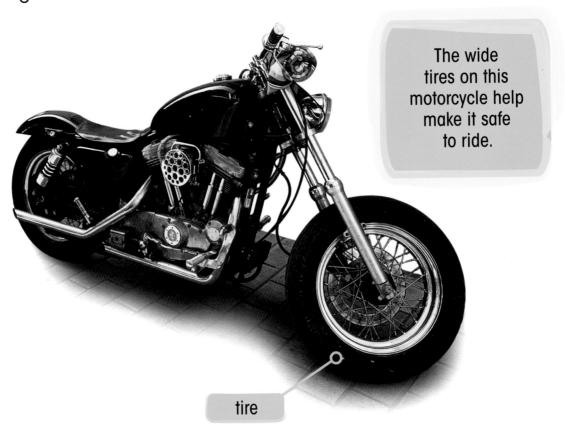

The wide tires on this motorcycle help make it safe to ride.

tire

This is the rear wheel
of a motorcycle.

A motorbike has an **engine** that makes the rear wheel turn. It is connected to the wheel with a chain. The engine needs **fuel** to make it work.

Old Motorbikes

This strange machine was one of the first motorbikes.

One of the first motorbikes was built in 1885 in Germany. It had a wooden frame and wooden wheels. Today's motorbikes are made mostly of metal and plastic.

This motorbike is called the
Silent Grey Fellow.

Around 1900, companies began making motorbikes for
people to buy. One of these motorbike companies was
Harley-Davidson. Harley-Davidson became one of the
most popular makers of motorbikes.

Classic Motorbikes

Classic motorbikes look good as well as feel good to ride.

A classic motorbike is an old motorbike that is famous because of the way it looks. The Harley-Davidson 45 is a classic motorbike. It was made in the 1940s.

Collectors keep their classic motorbikes shiny and in perfect condition.

Many people enjoy collecting classic motorbikes. They spend hours repairing, cleaning, and polishing them. Collectors often display their bikes at classic motorbike shows.

Where Motorbikes Are Used

Most motorbikes are used on roads that have a smooth surface. Riding a motorbike is a good way of getting around quickly. Many people use them in busy towns and cities.

In countries where there are many people, motorbikes are useful for driving to work and school.

Motorbikes do not take up much space on a narrow road.

In some places, roads are very narrow. It is hard for cars to drive along these roads. Motorbikes are a good way to get around these places.

Mopeds

A moped is like a bicycle with a small **engine** attached. Mopeds are cheap to buy and easy to use. Riders often use a moped when they are first learning to ride a motorbike.

Mopeds are smaller than other motorbikes.

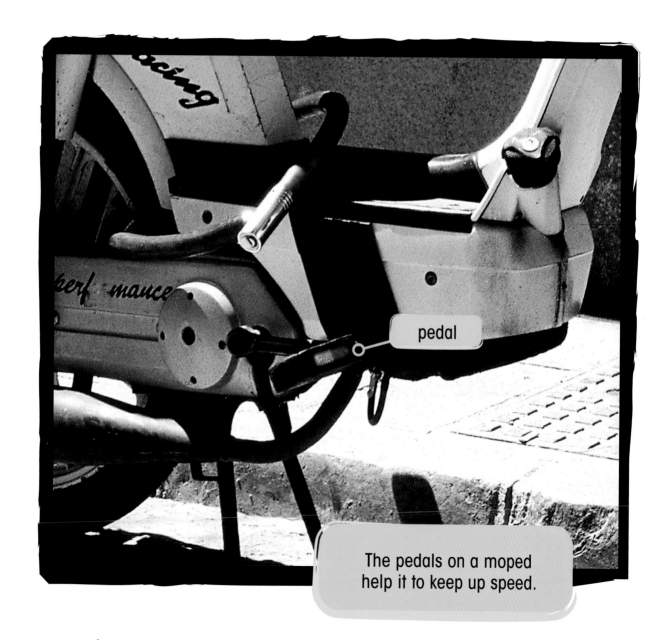

pedal

The pedals on a moped
help it to keep up speed.

A moped has pedals like the pedals on a bicycle.
The rider pedals to start the engine. The pedals
also give extra power when going up steep hills.

Scooters

A scooter has much smaller wheels than a normal motorbike. Many people ride scooters to get to work. In some countries, teenagers ride them for fun.

Scooters can be small, but they can still carry two people.

engine

The small engine on a scooter means that it is good for going short distances.

A scooter has a small **engine** next to the rear wheel. The engine moves the scooter by making the rear wheel turn. The rider's seat is above the engine.

Superbikes

Riders can race against each other on very powerful motorbikes called superbikes. These bikes can ride along at nearly 185 miles (300 kilometers) per hour.

Superbikes have large engines and can go very fast.

helmet

knee pad

Riders lean their superbikes over to help them go around corners.

A superbike's wide, rounded **tires** give plenty of grip to stop it from skidding. The riders wear special clothing, such as pads to protect their knees.

Find Out More

Graham, Ian. *Motorbikes.* Chicago: Raintree, 2006.

Hill, Lee Sullivan. *Motorcycles.* Minneapolis, MN: Lerner, 2004.

Tiner, John Hudson. *Motorcycles.* Mankato, MN: Creative Education, 2004.

Index